CRIME SCENE INVESTIGATION

FINGERPRINT FORENSICS

BY DONNA McKINNEY

BLASTOFF! DISCOVERY

LASTOFF! DISCOVERY, AN IMPRINT OF BELLWETHER MEDIA BY FLUTTERBEE

Blastoff! Discovery launches a new mission: reading to learn. Filled with facts and features, each book offers you an exciting new world to explore!

This edition first published in 2027 by Bellwether Media, Inc.

For information regarding permission, write to Bellwether Media, Inc., Attention: Permissions Department,
3500 American Blvd W, Suite 150, Bloomington, MN 55431.

Library of Congress Cataloging-in-Publication Data is available at www.loc.gov or upon request from the publisher.

ISBN: 9798898800796 (hardcover)
ISBN: 9798898802035 (ebook)

Editor: Rachael Barnes   Series Designer: Josh Brink

Printed in the United States of America, North Mankato, MN.

TABLE OF CONTENTS

WHAT IS FINGERPRINT FORENSICS?

Billions of people can be identified by patterns they carry everywhere they go. These patterns are known as fingerprints. They are formed by the tiny ridges in the skin on the tip of each finger. Every person's fingerprints are one of a kind!

Thousands of years ago, the people of Babylon used fingerprints in business. They pressed their fingertips into clay to record business deals. In the 1890s, police began using fingerprints to solve crimes. Today fingerprints are important **evidence** for **crime scene investigators** (CSIs).

THEY ONLY LOOK ALIKE!

Not even identical twins have the same fingerprints!

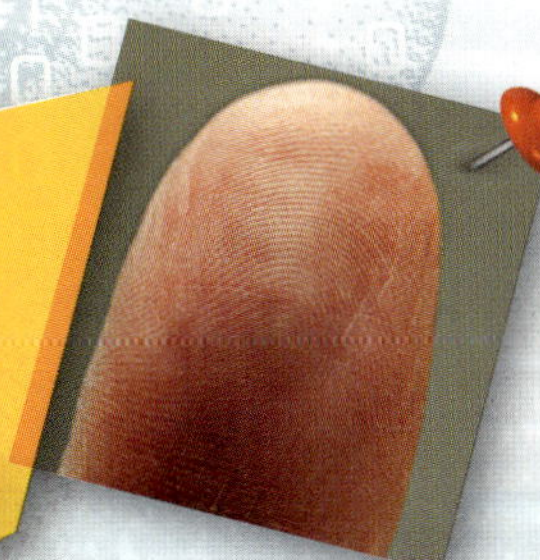

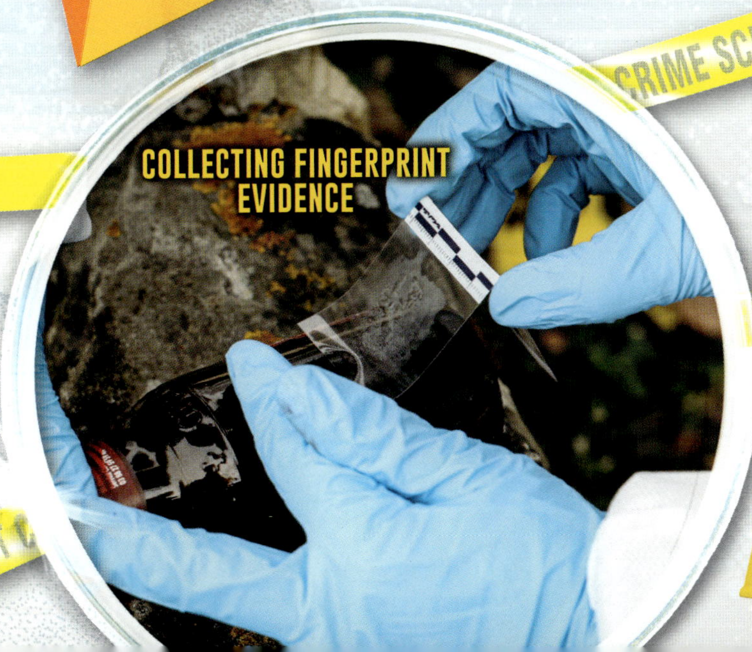

CSIs search for different types of fingerprints. Visible prints can be left by fingers covered in dirt, ink, or blood. Plastic prints are visible on soft surfaces, such as bars of soap. Latent prints cannot be seen easily. These prints are left by sweat and oil on the skin.

Biometrics are the measurements of a person's physical features. These can be used to identify a person. Fingerprints are a type of biometric. CSIs send fingerprints from crime scenes to **forensic scientists**. These scientists use tools to test and identify fingerprints. Fingerprints can link a **suspect** to a crime scene.

PLASTIC PRINT

STATS

FBI FINGERPRINT RECORDS

over **190 million** records as of 2026

TIME NEEDED TO SEARCH PAPER RECORDS

over **one month**

TIME NEEDED TO SEARCH DIGITAL RECORDS

10 seconds or less

FINGERPRINT COLLECTION

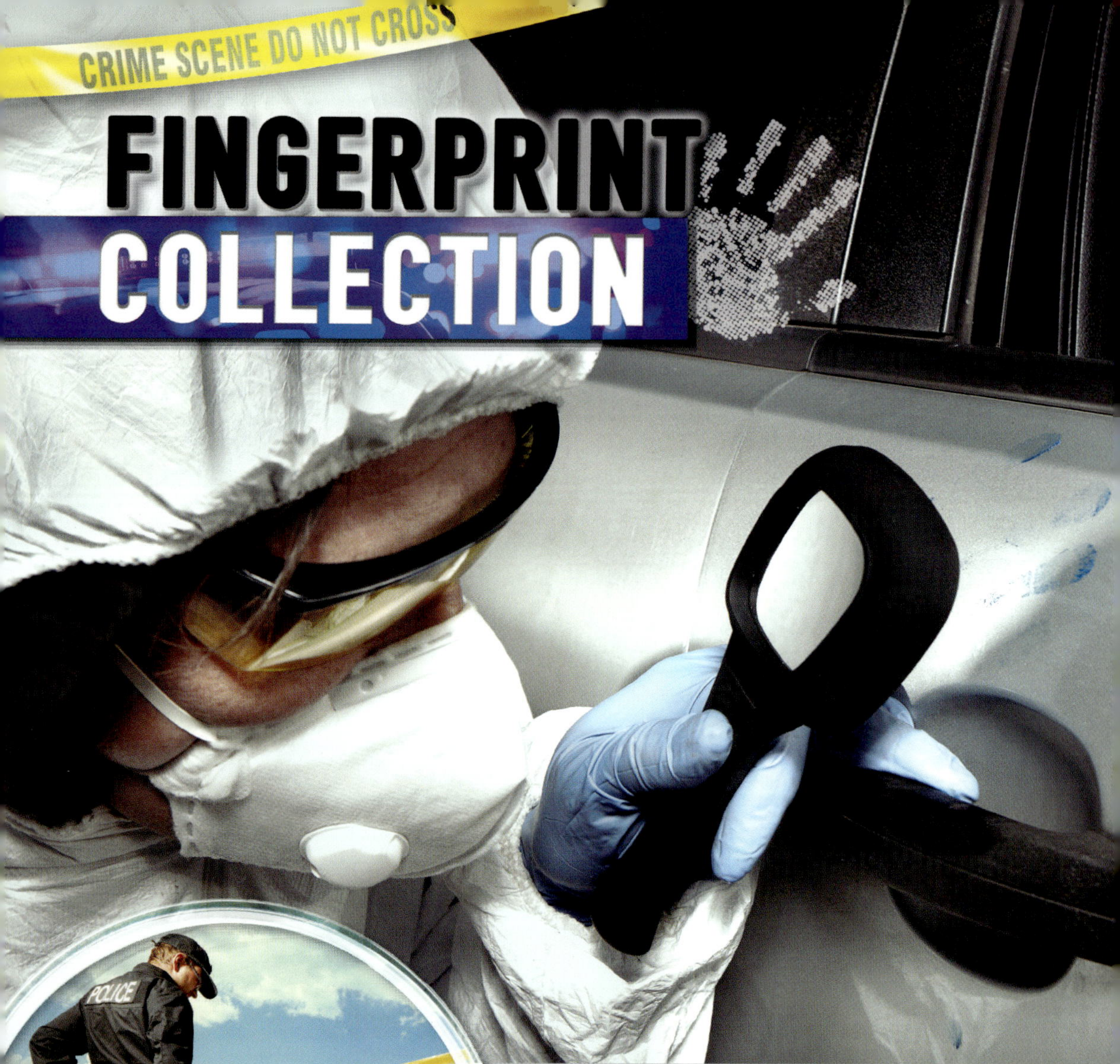

CSIs collect fingerprints and other evidence at crime scenes. Larger police departments have CSIs on their team. Smaller departments train regular police officers to collect prints.

At the crime scene, CSIs wear gloves. This keeps them from putting their own prints on objects. Usually a team works the scene. They divide the scene into sections. They search for fingerprints and other evidence such as hair, fibers, or shoe prints.

CSIs look carefully for visible and plastic fingerprints. To find latent prints, CSIs often use a process called dusting. They dust objects with powder. The powder makes prints visible. CSIs test surfaces at the scene that are likely to have latent fingerprints, such as door handles and countertops.

SPECIAL TAPE

Some of the tape CSIs use shows if the person who left the print had recently handled illegal drugs or explosives.

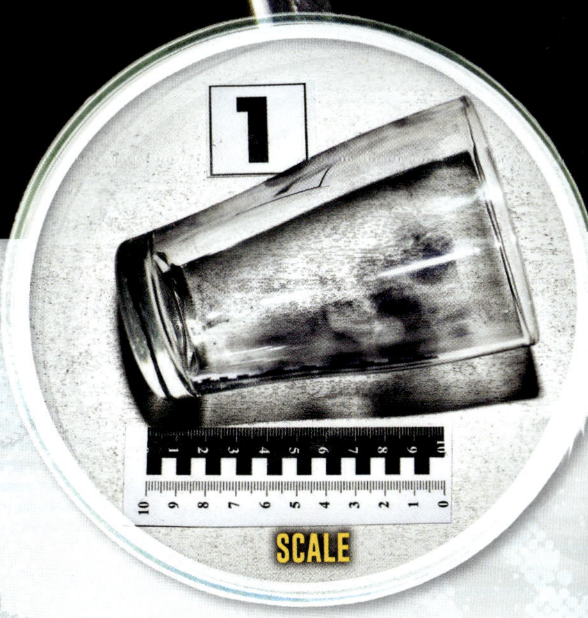

CSIs photograph the prints. A marker or scale may be placed next to fingerprints. Photos are taken as evidence before anything is moved at the scene. CSIs may "lift," or pick up, latent prints from the surface with clear tape.

Besides dusting, CSIs can find prints by shining a powerful light. These lights allow CSIs to see latent prints. They can also apply superglue **vapors** to the prints. These glue fumes stick to prints and make them visible.

CSIs use chemicals to see prints on paper. The chemicals turn the prints purple. Now they can be seen and photographed.

CSIs record fingerprint evidence. They write details on an index card about where the prints were found. They place lifted prints on the card. Later, they write a more detailed report.

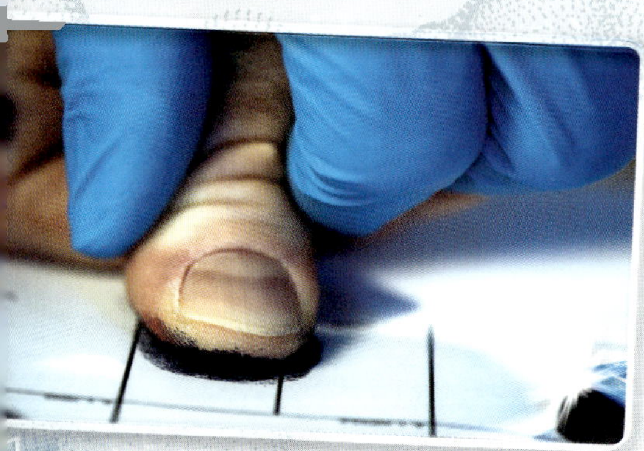

Fingerprints are also collected from specific people. This is done for certain jobs or as part of an arrest. Fingerprints were once recorded by inking a person's fingertips and pressing the inked fingers onto paper. Police kept paper records of the prints. Using paper records to find print matches took a long time.

AUTOMATED FINGERPRINT IDENTIFICATION SYSTEM (AFIS)

YEAR INVENTED

1974

AFIS IN 1989

WHAT IS IT?

AFIS is a database that forensic scientists and police use to search for fingerprint records. It can search through a billion records in 10 seconds or less!

By 1999, technology had greatly advanced. Police began capturing fingerprints electronically with a scanner. Fingerprints were stored digitally for the first time! They are stored in the Automated Fingerprint Identification System (AFIS). Both the Federal Bureau of Investigation (FBI) and state police departments use AFIS.

CRIME SCENE DO NOT CROSS

SOLVING THE CRIME

FORENSIC LABORATORY

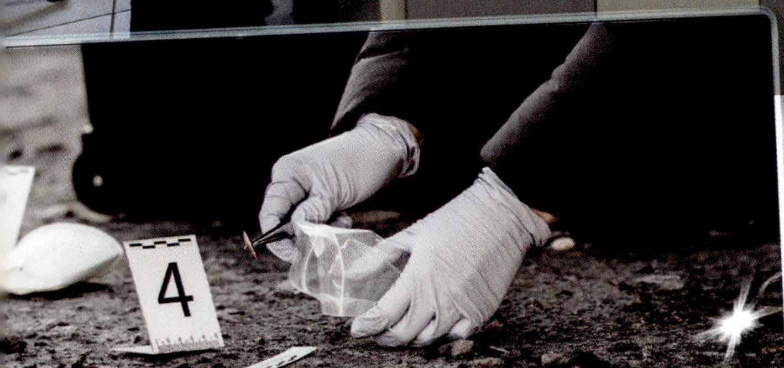

CSIs send collected fingerprints to a **forensic laboratory**. There, forensic scientists study the prints. They are trained in fingerprint **analysis**.

The methods scientists use to examine fingerprints have changed. In the early days, they relied on magnifying glasses called loupes. Loupes are still used today to see small print details. But computers are now a larger part of fingerprint analysis. Computers scan prints. They allow forensic scientists to analyze prints digitally. This method helps scientists work faster.

EXPERT USING A LOUPE, 1920S

CASE FILE

MARTIN LUTHER KING JR.

CRIME assassination of Martin Luther King Jr.

YEAR OF THE CRIME 1968

HOW IT WAS SOLVED An assassination is a sudden murder for political reasons. Investigators of this assassination found fingerprints on the weapon and a map used to plan the crime. The fingerprints matched a criminal in the FBI fingerprint records. The case was solved!

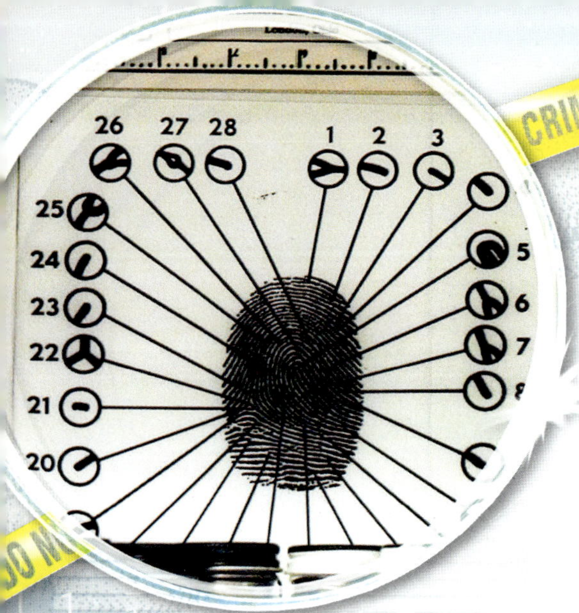

Forensic scientists study the patterns of ridges in the fingerprint. They also study tiny details called **minutiae**. They compare crime scene prints to those in state or FBI **databases**.

CASE FILE

CRIME murder of Carroll Bonnet

YEAR OF THE CRIME 1978

HOW IT WAS SOLVED

Investigators collected fingerprints and other evidence from the crime scene. No fingerprint matches were found at the time. In 2008, a search in the Integrated AFIS (IAFIS) database found a match. This evidence helped solve a 30-year-old case!

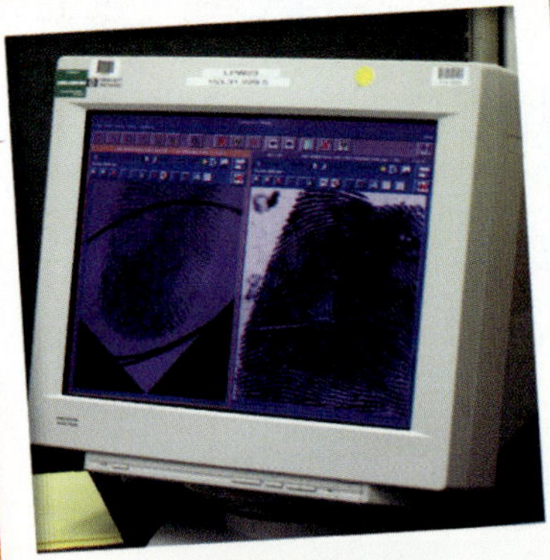

IAFIS DATABASE

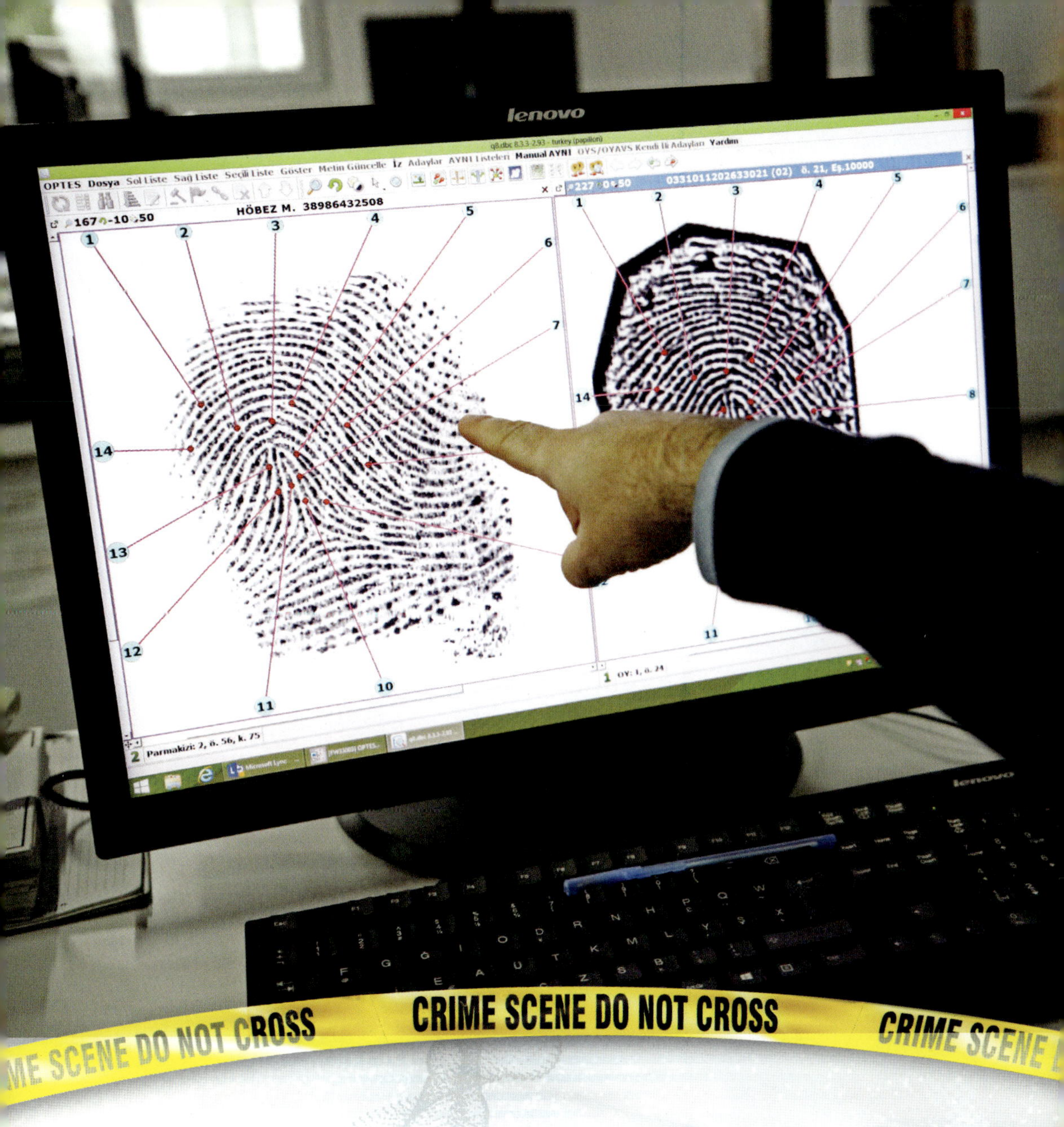

AFIS and similar tools produce lists of potential matches. Scientists look for an exact match from that list. But it can be hard to match prints correctly. Some prints are smudged. Others only show part of the print. Even well-trained scientists can struggle to make a correct match.

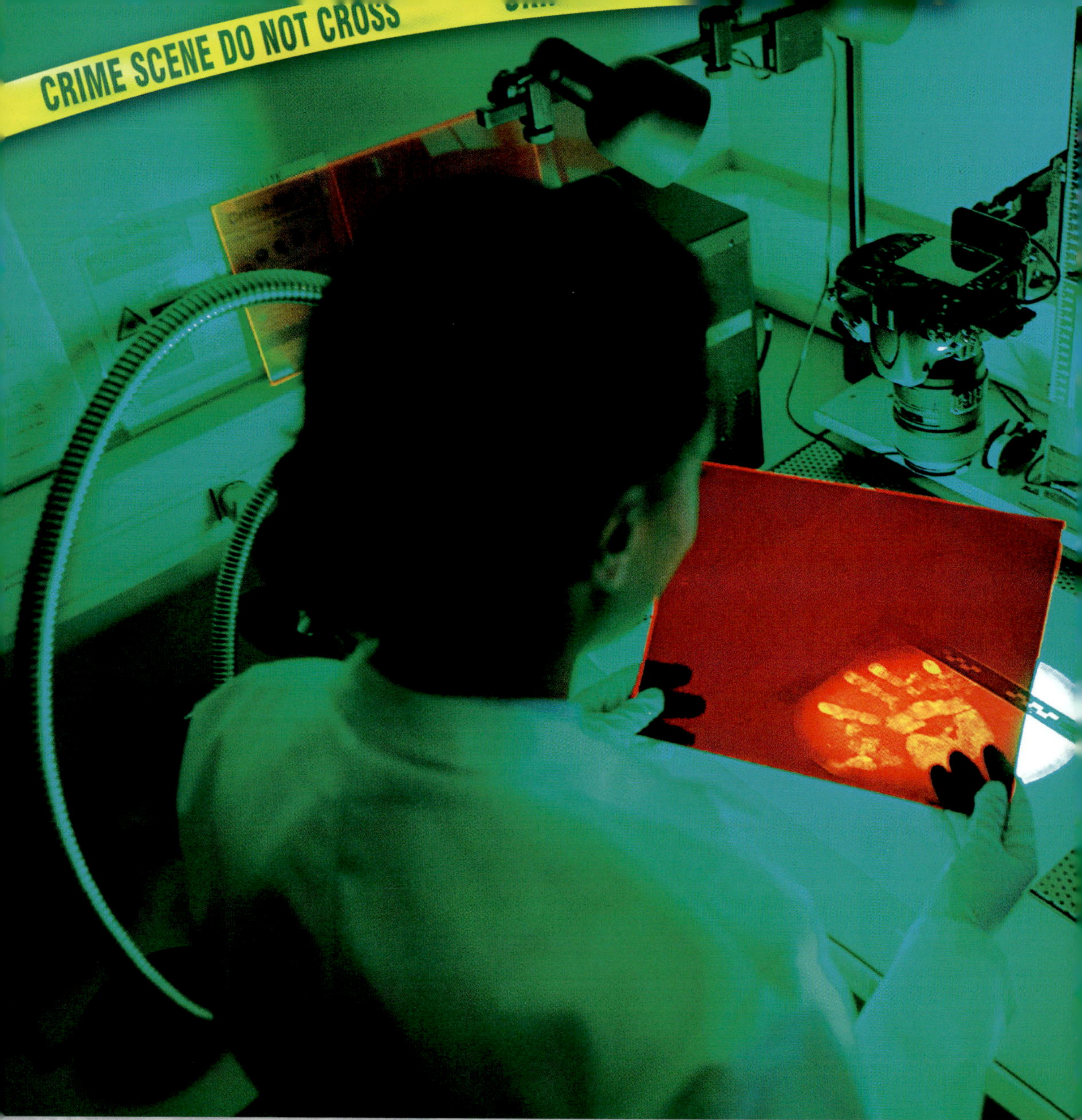

Forensic scientists use the **ACE-V method**. First, they decide if prints are good quality. Usable prints are studied. Scientists note important patterns and minutiae. Then they compare the crime scene prints to the potential matches.

FINGERPRINTS IN THE WILD

Humans are not the only animals with fingerprints. Monkeys, apes, and koalas have fingerprints too.

MONKEY FINGERPRINTS

Next, scientists evaluate if the crime scene print is a match to a database print. The final step in the method is verification. Another forensic scientist examines the prints. That person also uses the ACE-V method to confirm the result.

Forensic scientists then document their conclusion. They might decide that the prints are inconclusive. This means there is not enough information to confidently say a suspect was at a crime scene. Scientists may conclude there is a match. Matches connect suspects to the scene of the crime. This is called identification.

Scientists write a report about the analysis process and the results. They send this information to the investigators working on the case.

FINGERPRINT EXPERT AT A TRIAL

Later, the forensic scientist may serve as an expert witness in a trial. Lawyers present the evidence. The scientist presents the findings about the fingerprints involved in the case. Lawyers can ask the scientist questions.

Fingerprints are an important piece of evidence to solve crimes. But fingerprints alone are usually not enough to **convict** a person. They are used along with other evidence to prove a person is guilty. A judge or jury decides the case.

THE FUTURE OF FINGERPRINTING

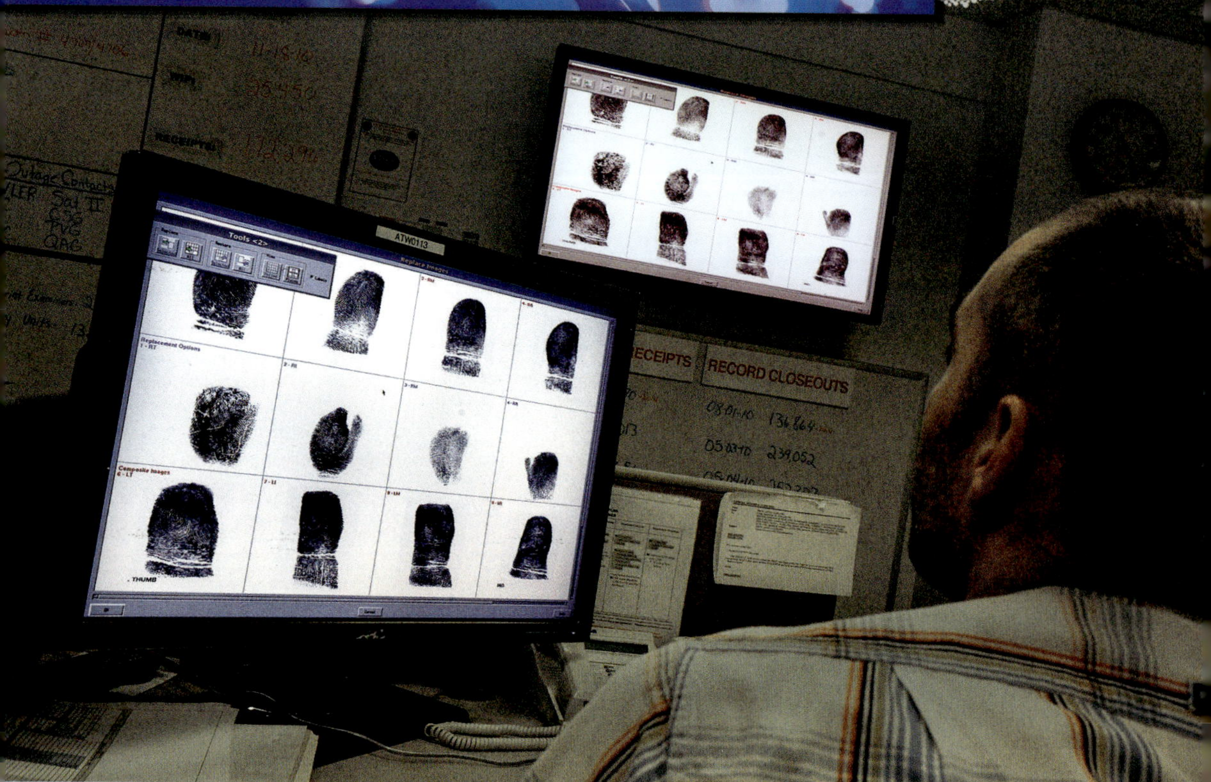

Better tools and technology are making fingerprint forensics faster and more accurate. Researchers are developing better imaging devices. CSIs will be able to take higher quality fingerprint images. The images can be processed at crime scenes. Busy forensic laboratories can take months to process prints. This digital analysis will take minutes.

Another tool is the FBI's Next Generation Identification (NGI) system. NGI records several biometrics, including fingerprints. The system's searches are more accurate than earlier systems. NGI also allows CSIs to do fast searches of fingerprints at crime scenes.

RISKS WITH PROGRESS

Large databases of biometrics can be hard to keep secure. Fingerprints and other personal information can be stolen.

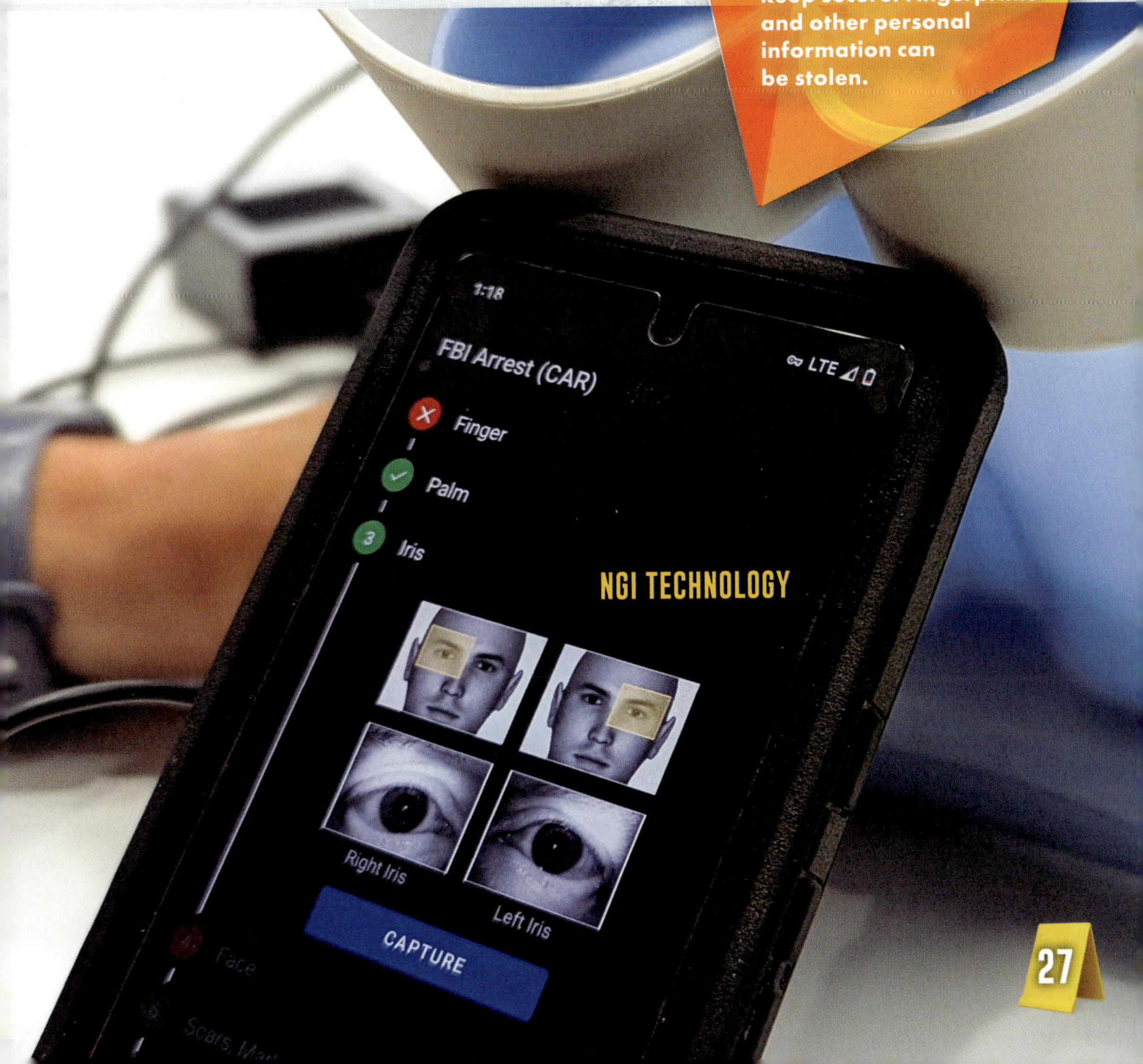

NGI TECHNOLOGY

Artificial intelligence (AI) is now used to analyze fingerprints. AI can find and match print patterns. It works faster and more accurately than humans. If a crime scene print is smudged, AI can help with that too. AI enhances the print image, making it easier to find the right matches.

CHALLENGES

POOR QUALITY PRINTS

HUMAN ERROR

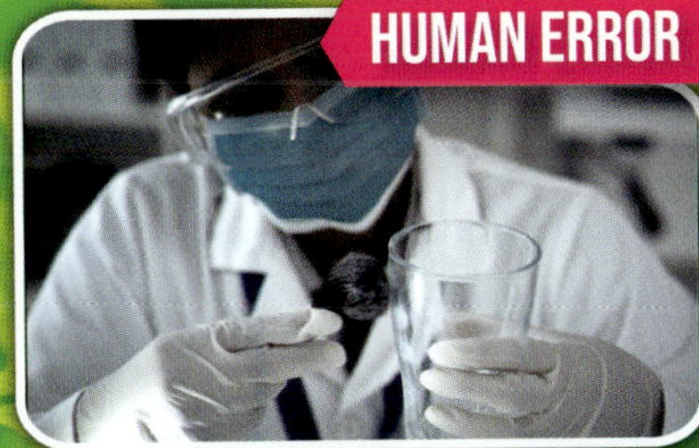

BIASED AI RESULTS

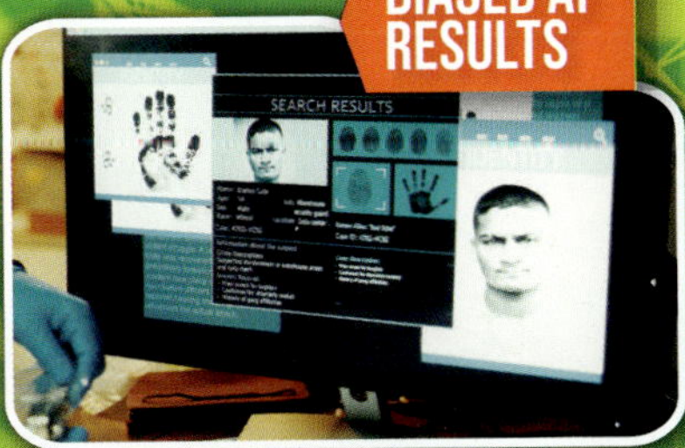

TOO MANY FINGERPRINT RECORDS

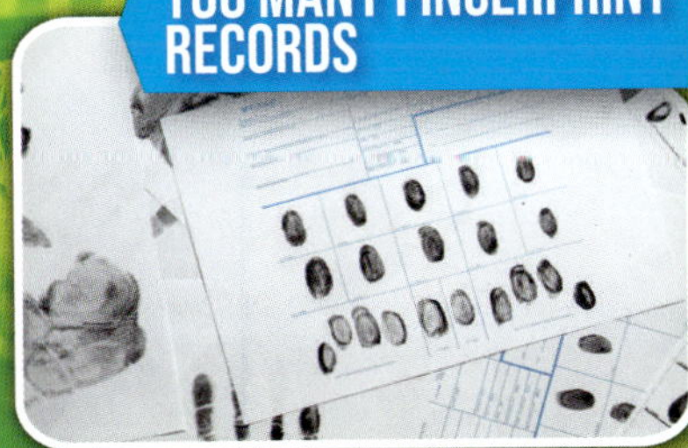

AI can also connect fingerprints to other biometric data. This allows police to more accurately identify suspects. But AI results can be **biased**. Scientists are still needed to draw final conclusions about print matches.

Improving fingerprinting from collection to analysis creates more concrete evidence to track down criminals. Case closed!

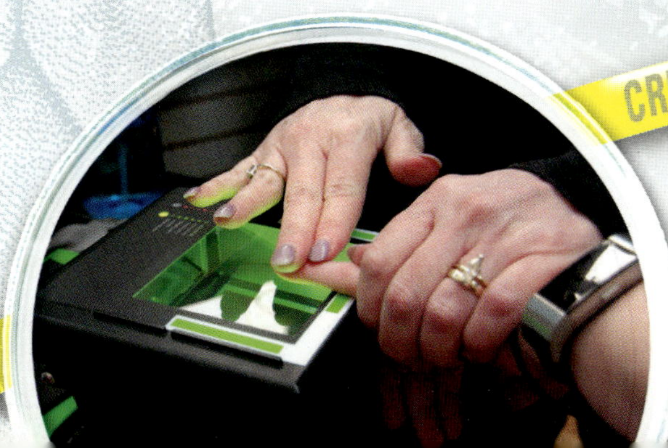

GLOSSARY

ACE-V method–a method used to draw a conclusion about fingerprint matches; ACE-V stands for analysis, comparison, evaluation, and verification.

analysis–the process of looking carefully at something to understand and identify its important parts

artificial intelligence–a computer's ability to do things a human mind can do

biased–giving results that favor certain characteristics or outcomes

biometrics–the measurements of a person's physical features; biometrics can be used to identify people through their fingerprints, their facial features, or their voice.

convict–to find someone guilty of a crime

crime scene investigators–people who collect and analyze evidence found at crime scenes

databases–digital systems used to store and sort data

evidence–a witness statement or an item or impression found at a crime scene that links a suspect to a crime

forensic laboratory–a place where scientists perform tests to study evidence left at a crime scene

forensic scientists–people who use scientific methods to study physical evidence

minutiae–the points where fingerprint ridges end or split

suspect–a person the police believe may have committed a crime

vapors–gases

TO LEARN MORE

AT THE LIBRARY

Campbell, Grace. *Fingerprints*. Minneapolis, Minn.: Lerner Publications, 2021.

Korte, Steve. *The Prints of Thieves: Batman & Robin Use Fingerprint Analysis to Crack the Case*. Mankato, Minn.: Capstone Publishing, 2017.

Ross, Melissa. *Forensics for Kids: The Science and History of Crime Solving with 21 Activities*. Chicago, Ill.: Chicago Review Press, 2022.

ON THE WEB

FACTSURFER

Factsurfer.com gives you a safe, fun way to find more information.

1. Go to www.factsurfer.com.
2. Enter "fingerprint forensics" into the search box and click 🔍.
3. Select your book cover to see a list of related content.

INDEX

The images in this book are reproduced through the courtesy of: Jim Thompson/ Albuquerque Journal/ Alamy Stock Photo, front cover; Jeff McCollough, pp. 2 (evidence marker 1), 3 (evidence marker 3); Uri, p. 3 (evidence marker 2); FRANCOIS LO PRESTI/ Stringer/ Getty Images, pp. 4-5; Octavian, p. 5 (fingerprint); ALAIN JOCARD/ Getty Images, p. 5 (fingerprint evidence); Couperfield, p. 6 (all); Denys, p. 7 (plastic print); Pixel-Shot, p. 7 (stats top); sebra, p. 7 (stats middle); Leonid Iastremskyi, p. 7 (stats bottom); Couperfield, p. 8 (all); Alsu, p. 9 (top); Sebastian Gollnow/ picture alliance/ Getty Images, p. 9 (bottom); FBI Media/ Federal Bureau of Investigation, pp. 10, 14 (bottom), 18 (bottom), 27; Dale A Stork, p. 11; franz12, p. 11 (bottom); D-Keine, pp. 12, 14 (iStock); Alisusha, p. 13 (top); NICOLAS TUCAT/ Stringer/ Getty Images, p. 13 (bottom); Bettmann/ Getty Images, p. 15 (top); Sendo Serra, p. 15 (bottom); Kosamtu, p. 16 (top); PRESSLAB, p. 16 (bottom); FPG/ Hulton Archive/ Getty Images, p. 17 (top); National Park Service/ Wikimedia Commons, p. 17 (bottom); JAY LAPRETE/ AP Newsroom, p. 18 (top); Serkan Avci/ Anadolu Agency/ Getty Images, p. 19; BSIP/ Universal Images Group/ Getty Images, pp. 20-21; Maryna Marchenko, p. 21 (top); Murrr Photo, p. 21 (bottom); Susan Tripp Pollard/ MediaNews Group/ East Bay Times/ Getty Images, p. 22; Валерия Стоганенко, p. 23 (top); pressmaster, p. 23 (bottom); Nikki Kahn/ The Washington Post/ Getty Images, pp. 24-25; sirtravelalot, p. 25; Michael S. Williamson/ The Washington Post/ Getty Images, p. 26; PAUL J. RICHARDS/ AFP/ Getty Images, p. 28; borzywoj, p. 29 (top left); PeopleImages, p. 29 (top right, middle left); New Africa, p. 29 (middle right); Cass, p. 29 (bottom).